Fire Body Warm
Ellie Ann Deighton

Copyright © 2025 by Ellie Ann Deighton

All rights reserved.

No part of this publication may be reproduced, distributed, or transmitted in any form or by any means, including photocopying, recording, or other electronic or mechanical methods, without the prior written permission of the publisher, except as permitted by Australian copyright law. For permission requests or bulk orders, contact the author.

The story, all names, characters, and incidents portrayed in this production are fictitious. No identification with actual persons (living or deceased), places, buildings, and products is intended or should be inferred.

Book Cover by Ellie Ann Deighton

1st Edition 2025

Contents

Epigraph	1
Ellie's Fires	2
Dedication	5
Foreword	7
1. Fire is the star.	11
2. Fire is the spark.	17
3. Fire is the chaos.	51
4. Fire is the hearth.	63
Fire After Dark [Adults Only]	89
Water River Run	107
About the author	109
Author's note	111
Acknowledgements	113

Fire Body Warm is a journey into the depths of the life force that lives inside you,
That is you,
That breathes you,
And the ways you have limited that fire's expression since you landed Earth-side.
Wherever you believe you came from,
For the sake of the book let us agree it was from the stars

For there was a fire
And it landed in your body
And you went cold
But you were born to be warm.
~ evidence suggests

ELLIE'S WILDFIRES

FICTION
Ankhara Codes I: An Adventure to Essence
Ankhara Codes II: Allies of the Soul
Ankhara Codes III: A Devotion To Peace

ORACLE CARDS
Fruits of the Feminine

POETRY
'It' is GOLD
Silver Witch Rose
Water River Run

NON-FICTION
Myths of a Mystic Woman

JOURNAL
Creatively Loving

MUSIC ALBUMS
Temple Calling: An Album For Your Altar
Heart Calling: A Love Anthology (coming 2025)

ONLINE TRAININGS & COURSES:
Intuitively Me: The Wheel of Life

more at elliedeighton.com

This is the second book of seven in The Elemental Collection; a poetry series focused on the seven essential elements of fulfilment.

You can read The Elemental Collection in any order you choose.

Hello flame,
This is for you.
Your biggest fan,
Ellie

(Get it?)

ELLIE ANN DEIGHTON

Foreword
In my journal I wrote...

July 17 2024

End result: To meet my muse and be informed of the calling of my heart; Fire Body Warm.

I am the magic
And the muse
And I am here
To say to you:

It's time to feel
Between your legs
The woman you are
Or the man you've said
You'd love to love
Or be, or befriend
The person you are
When the day turns in.

It's time to remember
The dance between the sheets
That love is possibilities
It's stars, it's infinity
Don't you remember
The first time you felt alive?
And no, I don't mean as a baby
I mean as you grew, inside
I mean the way you felt when they looked in your eyes
And loved you for who you were
The way you felt when they held both your hands
And told you to be who you were
The way you felt when your love changed
And still you stayed connected
The way you felt when pleasure took hold
And you kept your heart at the centre
The way you remembered to come back to love
That time your heart was broken
And the way you remembered to keep looking up
When the ground was swallowing you open
The way you held your hand out to a child
And said, 'Check your body, you're okay,'
The way they laughed and ran around again
As soon as your smile was sent their way.
Can't you remember that we are all one
And we're crazy for thinking we're separate?
And madder still, to separate pleasure

From the ways that we're meant to be together.
It is a pleasure to love ourselves
Our friends, each other
The greatest pleasure to find that sweet union
That expresses our greatness together
So why then in shame must we shrink ourselves down
Limit this bliss of who we are?
Well, you see the answer is we mustn't,
And congratulations for getting this far
For you have come to this place, to read or write
this book
Because you can feel a warmth in your fire
You know there is something more than your looks
When you tap into your intimate desire
It's love and freedom and magic to cherish
It's everything it means to be human
And there's just no way, not a chance, not an
inkling,
That you aren't meant to love with freedom
So love and feel and burn and be free
And first undertake this remembering
Read all these pages and the spirit in between them
And allow the cold to be forsaken.

Welcome to Fire.

Fire is the star.

Burning

Is all I know

Burning and moving

And speeding up

There's no slowing down

There's only momentum

Moving

Growing

Going

Where am I going?

I don't know.

Who am I becoming?

There is a sense

Of playing the game

Of going into the greatest playground.

There is a woman

An egg meets a spermatozoa

A human is made

– When the fire starts, it burns

Oooooooft.

Hit

Like a plonk

Sudden

Like a force is knocked out of me

If I had a force it could be gone

If I had a breath it could be restricted

If I had...

If I...

If we...

– The star lost its sparkle in its very own body

I'm sliding

Slipping

Compressing

Forcing

Uncomfortable

Leaving

Why am I leaving?

I don't want to

It's warm here

Wonderful here

Familiar here

Good here

Right here

Home here

Good here

Right here

Home here

– The fire starts to scream

FIRE BODY WARM

I'm alive
And I'm limited
And it's part of being alive
And I don't know what to do with it
All I know
Is that I am alive
Helpless in the flesh
– A fire contained

ELLIE ANN DEIGHTON

Fire is the spark.

I'm just little
And nobody knows
But sometimes
When I'm alone
I touch myself
And I don't know where I learnt it
But I like how it feels
Until after
After it feels bad
Even though I'm alone
Even though nobody knows
Even though nobody is watching
It's as though everybody is
And everybody knows
That now I am dirty
And if anybody ever really did know
They wouldn't love me
I would be in so much trouble
And so I've learnt
And I've decided
And I don't remember when
And I have no concept of how
Only that it is true
That bodies aren't for touching
Unless somebody else tells you to
– The fire is releasing unknown sensations

I don't know these flames
They weave inside me
I'm not even aware they're there
But deep down I see the truth
I am these flames
That weave inside me
The adults aren't aware they're here
Deep down we are remembering
– The star says all humans have flames inside them

I wish I knew
What to do
What's okay
The other people coming
Don't know
That when I'm alone
And sometimes when I wake up from dreams
I feel good
I touch myself and it feels good
And it feels like such a terrible thing
To feel so good
And yet
It feels so good
And I don't know why
Mummy turns off the TV when people are kissing
But I thought only people who love each other kiss
So why is kissing hidden
And why is love shameful
And why is touching myself not okay?
– The fire burns through the middle

He doesn't know I like him
And she doesn't know I like her
They don't know I like them
And I don't know what I prefer
And somehow I feel like it matters
Even though Daddy says it don't
Somehow I feel I could love anybody
Sometimes I tell myself I won't
I don't know what's done to this body
I just know that I want to see
What's underneath all the covers
To figure out who I'm meant to be
But maybe who I'd like to be is bad
Maybe loving anybody is wrong
Because it seems to make so many people sad
'It's a shame,' they sing like a song
'It's a waste,' when he loves a he, not her
'It's a phase,' when she loves a she, not the
Embodiment of a father figure
Just for the love of a person
It's not meant to be like that
Why do I feel so different?
Everything is lost now
Friendships
Faith in family too
I see the pain in Mummy's friends' eyes
And still I can't see the difference
I don't see the difference between any of the loves

I just think they're all the same
But everything everyone else is saying
Tells me I'm wrong, it's a shame
It must be I'm wrong, it's a shame
It must be my song is a shame
It must be I am a shame
It must be my shame
– The fire is corrupt

On Sundays the door closes
We can't go in
No knocking unless it's an emergency
I don't know what they're doing
But I know they love each other
And I know it won't make happiness if we don't listen
And I know we all are happy after
And I know what goes on in there is a secret
And that's all I know
– Fire isn't meant to be a secret

There are books that show the babies
Where they started
And where they came from
And they've been slid over to me
They're mine to read now
I'm allowed to
I'm a big girl now
I'm basically an adult
I am so terrified I might get my period
I don't want to go to the toilet
And at school I always go in with friends
Because we fear the moment
We fear the blood
There's no such thing as sacred
I've never heard of a rite of passage
I just know one day I'll see it
There in my underwear
An everlasting intruder that will change me forever
And I've got more pubes than all my friends
So maybe
Someone says
I will bleed first
And then I will be all alone
Waiting
For another friend to bleed
And isn't that such a bad place to be,
Waiting for a friend to bleed?
It sounds horrible

Like a place I don't want to go

And yet I'll go to the toilet

Because I have to

And I'm always scared

Because soon I'll have no other choice

But to be different

From everyone I've ever loved

And suddenly no one will know me

And I'll harbour this secret

And worse

I'll have to tell my mum

– Flames can fan the fire, shame can tame it

I wonder

If she'll notice

If I don't tell her

Of course she will

But maybe she won't

And maybe I can get away with the secret

Maybe there's nothing wrong

Maybe I'm dying

I'm pretty sure it's selfish

So I won't tell anyone

And later

Maybe later

I'll let her know I'm dying

– Fire in a woman means bleeding

I feel like
The other half
Already knows something I don't
And it's best I don't know
I'm told I don't want to
They separated us
Apparently over there is for women's business
But what if I marry a woman?
What if I want to be a woman?
What if I want to learn about the woman?
I guess I will never know their secrets
If someone says womb I'll scream
If someone says period I'll pretend I didn't hear
– The flame gets smaller with ignorance

I don't know
The body doesn't know
Who becomes it
Who touches it
Right?
But how come when that person touches me
My body opens
And when that person comes near to me
My body feels frozen
And how come it's weird
When that person hugs me
And sad if another person doesn't
And how come some things feel good some days
And other days, just no
And sometimes the shift happens in just moments
It was good
And then terrible and I want it to stop
And somehow I can't say that out loud
Like I've already said yes
And you can't stop an avalanche
'You can't turn boys on and off,' they said
But what if I turn off? What then?
Do I have to keep going?
Do I do what I can to speed it up?
I'll never know
Maybe I'll know when I have another go
– Sexual curiosity is a fire that can be nurtured or tortured

FIRE BODY WARM

How many times can I?
This feeling,
This explosion
It comes and comes and comes
And then goes
And if I keep trying
It kind of hurts
But if I just keep going
It really doesn't hurt
It's really good
Until it's over and I feel so tender
It's tender down there
Sensitive on other parts of me too
And a secret
A desperate secret
A shameful one
And I just can't stop
Because I want another
– How do people sleep once the fire starts exploding?

It's a rise like nothing has ever risen before
And then a fall so far
Like when you fall in a dream
And you wake up shocked in bed
Except here you just keep falling
And shame doesn't have a floor
– Fire is meant to move but we don't know what we don't know

I'll try that
It looks like it'll go in
I'll be able to wash it
I'm sure that's fine
I hope the lid doesn't come off
And I can shake the smell off it
Maybe I should spray it with deodorant?
Maybe it's not the best idea
I'll put it in anyway
See what happens
It feels amazing
I can't believe I'll never be able to tell anyone
– There are better toys to stoke the spark

Safety

That's what they taught us about

As if it's all a danger

Every spot could be a cancer

Every hair could carry lice

Rip it off

Rip off the hair

It's safer

More desirable

See what happens without it

It's smooth for a few moments at least

Shave it

Immediately

Cut off more

Change it

Make it look like this

No one will notice how wrong you are

If you do it right

But you'll still be wrong

Because this dangerous act is shameful

It will make you a baby

It will make you sick

No matter how you do it

But you're stupid if you don't know how it works

But you can't ask a question without being laughed at

And everybody wants to know

And some of us are too scared to use the internet to find out

And some of us see magazines in a box hidden in the shed

And some of us stumble across calendars
And some of us ripped open the sealed section
And some of us have been told
And all of us are scared shitless
Except those of us who abandoned ourselves and did it anyway
And those of us will pay for it later
We'll all pay for it later
– Fire ignorance is painfully expensive

I'm getting the picture
Getting that it works
In the world
That young ones shouldn't share their spark
Not this spark
Not this fire
Not this flame
And if they do
When they do
Inevitably
Because no one teaches us how to keep it in
And then the sparks fly
It spits out
It spills out
And before we know it
It's touched someone
We've touched someone
We've sparked their curiosity
And maybe it can be innocent
And harmless
And mean nothing
And maybe
It can be everything
It can be danger
It can be wrong
It can be unacceptable
It can be inappropriate
And somehow

Whatever it is
Even though nobody taught us
Even though it's seemingly natural
We've learnt that it's not
And somehow
No matter what the conditions
No matter the time and space
No matter the person
Somehow
And I can't explain it
We really can't explain it
And we really can't deny
That somehow
It even hurts to say
I don't want to say it
I feel dirty for it
I'm telling myself I'm wrong
I'm telling myself it's wrong to admit it
But that's the point
It has to be spoken to
It can't be kept in the shadow anymore
We can't pretend it isn't happening
We can't let them get away with it
We can't pretend nobody's home inside us
We have to own it
But nobody told us how
All I know is

If something goes wrong it's our fault
– If anyone's fire burns us, they'll say it's the fault of our spark

So I turned it off
I thought
It's not safe out there
There's nothing to be done
There's certainly nothing good to be done
There's nothing that can be okay about this
So the best thing
Is to pretend it doesn't exist
To laugh about it
To laugh at it
To pretend I don't want to
To pretend it doesn't happen
I wasn't touching, I was scratching
It didn't feel good, it was necessary
It wasn't pleasurable, it was functional
Am I supposed to be seeing this?
Is it funny that I want to read the book again?
Because I do want to learn about the body
It's curious growing bumps and hair
It's curious feeling differently
My emotions are all over the place
But I don't notice
Because I don't know what's normal
I just know I don't feel free
I just know I'm not free
I just know it's meant to be like *this*
This is how I'm meant to behave
This is how I'm meant to feel

This is what I'm meant to want
This is who I'm meant to say
Is okay and isn't
This is who can touch me
And *this* is who can't
And not because I say so
But because I've been told
This is how it is
This is dangerous
This is to be kept hidden
But
Fires aren't made for hiding
– Hidden fires are destructive

She said
Leave something to the imagination
And all I heard is,
Your body is bad
Hide your body
Put that away
Don't give them temptation
You're still a child
Those are yours but the world won't act like it
You can't be sovereign
You can't be what you want to be
Your expression is not okay
You're a dancer, but it must be a secret
You're a secret dancer
There's nothing you can do here that will keep you safePut more clothes on or you'll be in danger
Nobody realises how precious you are
And everybody realises how precious you are
So don't show them
Hold yourself back
Put it away
Put yourself away
Don't stand out
Standing out is dangerous
Visibility is dangerous
Be good and kind but not so kind they want you
Hold yourself back
Hold yourself back

Hold yourself back

– And somehow the whole world's fire became my responsibility

I couldn't turn it off
Even if I tried
And oh I tried
I even thought it was working
I even thought I'd get away with it
I even thought I would stay clean and good
And I was wrong
– The fire starts to burn

When it starts to burn again
It burns cold
Achingly cold

And then suddenly

As if it was never going to be contained
A rushing heat
Destructive and out of control
Like a volcanic explosion
And no one told me
Shutting it off would be impossible
They just made sure
I got it done
And it hurts so much to open
Even though I barely notice
And it hurts so much to close
Even though I pretend I like it
And it is so confusing to be me
Even though it seems I am happy
I wonder how many of us are pretending

I wonder

If I can seem as happy as this
And nobody knows the truth
Nobody sees what's really going on
And everybody acts as if nothing's the problem

But secretly everything is the problem
How the fuck does the world live
When everyone says we are meant to be closer to nature
But nobody lets nature move
– Fire body hurts

'*You are not alone*'
A little whisper on my shoulder
And it doesn't make sense
This voice I thought I had forgotten
It's right there with the fairies
Sending me messages
Telling me everything is going to be okay
Whispering to me softly
And yelling
Snapping me out of it when I need it
Everything is going to be okay
I can't explain it
Because there's all this fog
All this pain in the world
And somehow
It seems certain to me
Absolutely certain
Positively clear
That the only way I will ever ever ever
Live
Is freely
And right now
I can't imagine *how*
I can't imagine *where*
I can't imagine *who with*
I only know I will
Because the fire wants to burn

And all I want to do is let it
– Fire wins, best to roll with it from the inside

I've always learnt

And always thought that

Fire was on the outside

Fire was the way the world hurt

Fire was the way I could go get burnt

Fire was the energy with another person that I should avoid

At all costs

Because it holds the keys to every danger

Fire is to be mistrusted

Fire is to be shamed

Fire is to be shoved down

I really always thought a lot

And the thoughts were followed by all my feelings—

Desire

Shame

Grief

Anger

Confusion

Pleasure

Guilt

Confusion

Pleasure

Anger

Rage—

Make it stop

This is not okay

Everything is on all at once

Turn everything off

Don't touch me

I'm not loveable

This isn't right

Everything is wrong

You don't know what's going on with me

You've never been through this

You can't see the way I'm hurting

And maybe

It occurs to me

For the first time

They're all hurting too

– Fire doesn't want us to hurt, it tells us to live

If living ain't so bad,
Why is the fire?
If life ain't so bad,
Why do we shame the act that creates it?
I'm pretty sure
In fact my mum told me
So I'm certain
That is the way babies were made
And Mum also told me
The way I came into the world
Was the most painful
And most loving
Thing to ever happen
She told me
Her body ripped open
And then I was there
And suddenly her world was forever changed
And she said that was a good thing
She said
It didn't matter that it hurt
She was happy I made it
She was so happy she made me
She was so happy we were together
And so I get that it hurt
But she was happy
So why would the body dance that made that happen be a wrong thing?
How could making that happen ever be a wrong thing?

Why would anybody ever tell you or me
or any of the children or any of the adults
or even any of the nuns
That kind of love
Could be so terribly wrong
The kind of love that changed the world
Was also the love that shamed it.
I couldn't understand,
When a child is born
And everybody gawks at the innocence
And everybody laughs and smiles and cries the happy tears
How anybody
Could ever
Make that wrong
And yet I am certain
I can feel it in my bones
That there is nothing in the world
That could be more dangerous
– Fire is so confusing

Why can't someone teach me about the fire while looking into my eyes?
Why must they look away or down at the floor or up to the sky
As if praying for something to happen to take our attention away from the moment we are actually sharing in
Why can't someone look me in the eyes
And tell me they love me
And tell me this is how love works
And show me
Loving is okay
Your fire is simply your life
And your life wants to move
And life is meant to move
And there is nothing wrong with that
In fact
There is everything natural about that
And natural is the way
Natural is who we were born to be
And every human loves
And everything human is happier if they let the love
And the judgement bleed
Let it be and let it go
To let the love lead
Because really
Love leads the fire
It's the shame that squashes it
– Fire fans the love and the love fans the fire

Fire is the chaos.

They didn't know I was touching myself
But I was
And I kept going
I don't know what possessed me on this day
But I let my hand keep moving
And it was a secret
Nobody knew
I barely even knew myself
It has become unconscious by this point you see
Maybe because I've accepted it
Likely because I've pretended it isn't happening
So I'm touching myself
And I notice
Suddenly
It feels different
It feels so much better
And then it feels beyond
Like nothing I've ever felt before
Like nothing I've ever imagined
Suddenly
An explosion occurs
My body swollen
Throbbing in its most private, secret parts
I am sweating
It's hard to keep the secret
I want to breathe heavily and make sound
But I don't
Partially because it's a secret

And mostly because it is a complete shock
It feels...
Amazing
Like sunshine
And stars
At the same time
And the sun is spreading all over my skin
And the stars are exploding
And everything disappears
It's all okay
Everything feels at once at peace
And everything is all okay
And it keeps going
And I keep moving my hand
I keep letting it
And then the wave slows down
As if the sun slowly sets
And I can feel my heart rate speed through my whole body
And I can see the new quiet that has fallen over me
Like literally
I can see it
The air is sparkling
For a moment
And then the whole world crashes into me
And everything stops
My heart drops into my feet
And I think I accidentally tread upon it
And it squashes

And I feel sick
What was that?
What have I done?
Why do I want to do it again?
Why do I feel so terrible?
It's as though for one moment I was with God,
If God even exists
Of which I am wildly uncertain,
But if there is a God
I just met them
And then as quickly as it happened
As if it never happened
The God was gone
– All that was left after the first firework was shame

I cried that night
When nobody was looking
It had been an accident
And I wanted to do it again.
It felt so wrong that I wanted to do it again.
I cried shame filled tears
And they were heavy on my face
And I didn't know
If I would ever cry in the light ever again
I didn't know if I would ever be okay
I didn't know if what was happening was normal
I just knew I couldn't tell anybody
Like it was a secret that would kill me if I kept it
And torture me if I revealed it
And somehow revealing it seemed worse
So I cried myself to sleep silently
– Shaming the fire taught me to be quiet

When I realised it was an orgasm I felt silly

And equally

Profoundly proud that I'd figured it out

It was my body after all

So I should figure the things out

Learn about all the bits and pieces

And yet still

Somehow

I made it wrong

Still

Even though now I was hearing it was a good thing

And that people yearn for them

And it's what lovers want for each other

And apparently everybody masturbates

It doesn't matter

The damage is done now

But I don't see it as damage

I see it as self-preservation

No matter what

I must be quiet

No one must know

It must be a secret

That I must never show

And somehow

It's all everyone is talking about

It's all the boys want to do

And the girls are all talking about kisses

What's the difference between upstairs and downstairs kisses?

Why do some of us talk about love
And some of us talk about sex
As if it has to be different
And yet it's one and the same
Because none of us are allowed to cuddle
Cuddles lead to sex
Everybody knows
Don't lead anybody on
Don't tell the truth
Don't let anyone inside
Don't let anyone see you
Don't let anyone else dance with your body
Even if you want to
Even if you love them
Because it won't mean love
It'll mean something else
– Fire has been twisted

I saw him
And I couldn't contain myself
I wanted... in
And I couldn't explain it
I just knew
I felt he was pretty on the inside
He made me tingle
Just by looking at him
And the butterflies in my stomach had a party
I felt nervous
And he walked up to me
And he had already made me his girlfriend
And I couldn't understand
Why was this miracle happening?
And then he walked straight up to me
It may have been a dare
And kissed me
And it wasn't on my cheek
It was on my lips
And everybody screamed
And what they didn't see
Is the simultaneous joy and panic
Flipping like angry dancing partners on the inside of my chest
My chest hurt
Even though I smiled and placed a hand over my lips
And he cuddled me and told me he loved me
And I'm sure this is what my fairy tales told me would happen
And I can't understand why I'm scared

Do I let myself try to understand?
I think not.
I think no.
I think be grateful for what I get.
I think get over myself, this is what I daydreamed would happen
I think dreams really do come true
I think dreams aren't what I imagined them to be
I think I can create anything
I think it may be dangerous if I don't understand
And I'll never understand
So I'll pretend
It'll be like a dance I need to happen
Everything will be okay
But I don't believe what I tell myself
I am all confusion
One hundred percent
And fifty percent happy
I've become one hundred and fifty percent today
Enough stress for a whole extra person lives here
And that's the way it is
And six weeks later he dumped me
And the world ended
– Fire starts and hurts

Why do my friends and I love the same person?
Why does it hurt like this?
Why must we be pitted against one another?
Why have we swapped boyfriends?
Why do we think it's funny?
Does love really happen like this?
I don't know.
I don't know.
I want to show everyone that I know everything.
I think I know everything.
I know nothing.
– Nothing makes sense when the fire is made foreign

Why do some people seem good to like
And some people seem bad to like
Why are some crushes celebrated
Accepted
Everybody has them
And the rest are secrets
The rest are fields ready for rejection
In fact they all are
Even the ones we all share
None of us believe we can have them
None of us even imagine we'll ever hold hands
We're colluding in the rejection
Making each other feel better
What if crushes weren't bad or good?
What if they just were?
What if the crushes had the air to breathe?
What if I let my body feel its own way?
What if everything was okay and everything would work out?
I'm starting to think differently
But it seems no one else is
That makes it time to stop
– Fire wrecking is lonely

Once upon a time I had my first orgasm
And everybody changed
And everybody stayed the same
And nobody knew
But I did
And I've never felt more amazing
But then I've never felt more stuck
– Fire is meant to be free

Fire is the hearth.

Having your heart and sharing it too
They said it couldn't happen
They said I couldn't walk through the flames and return
They said I couldn't rise like the phoenix
They said I wasn't a bird
They said I couldn't burn slowly over time,
It had to be hard and fast
Like the movies where they taught us
Everyone triggers their love
And hurts them
And then it's their duty to forgive
Even if they're not okay with it
There was what they said it would be like
And then there was what it was like
When you walked through the door
And I really saw you
The real you
The soul of you
And a light turned on inside me
And it wasn't sexual
But it was erotic
And it wasn't about you
But it was inspired by you
Brighter with you
But it was my light
It was me turning on
It was me noticing the love that could be
Burning hot and bright and slow and warm all at once

FIRE BODY WARM

It was you
Who put your hand on my cold stomach
And waited for the warmth
To see when it came
Because you expected it
You expected the love to be communicated through your hands
Not because you expected an emptying out of me
Or crossing of my boundaries blindly
But because you were filled with love
And it meant I could love you the way I was born to
I could put my hands on you and allow the love to swell
There was no hurry
And every anticipation
There was no rush
And every desire
There was no need
And every love
Of every inch
And the lava melted through me
And the light was white hot
And it burned in you
But it didn't burn you
And it burned in me
But it didn't burn me
And when our lights wove together for the first time
They didn't get lost in one another
They simply watched in awe as the other danced brighter
And then we became one

Both lights become one
Not because we lost ourselves
But because we lost our Selves
The identity dissolved
The body melted
Warm in the fires of flesh
And then there was only the light
And then we held each other as our bodies fell back together
– Ashes to flesh, a reimagining of fire

They didn't tell me
That I could love in a way that made me feel calm
They told me
Love was meant to burn the house down
Tear apart everything I've ever known
Be the best personal development investment
Which should terrify me
Prepare me
To empty myself
To never be myself again
It's not me anymore
It's us
We have friends
I don't
We have a house
I don't
We have a home
I don't
We have a habit
I don't
We have a function
I don't
We have a purpose
I don't
We have a child
I don't
We have a body
I don't

ELLIE ANN DEIGHTON

We have a choice
I don't
They told me the flames would consume me
– The real flames brought me home

When the house burnt down
From the fires before
There was a moment of sheer fear
A letting go by accident
I didn't want this
It hurts
I fell
As if I had been holding on for a lifetime
Because I had
Because holding on was what I was meant to do
Holding on was my job
But all the houses kept burning down
No matter what I did.
Have no boundaries
And watch it burn
Have all the boundaries
And watch it burn
Have just one love
And watch it burn
Have multiple loves
And watch it burn
Have a Sunday love
And watch it burn Monday
Have a February love
And watch it burn in March
Have a year long love
And watch it burn in a day
And I had to realise

I had to acknowledge
That real love doesn't burn houses down
Not really
It might remodel them
It might move
It might shapeshift completely
You might live in different rooms
But the home need not be destroyed
The hearth need not be watered
Let it simply burn
Warm like a candle vigil
Reminding you of the love that lives here
Letting you hold onto the soul of this love
No matter the circumstance
No matter the furniture
The candle, still it burns
And the candle can burn to the base
And you can light a new one
And it's not painful,
It's refreshing
And the wax can melt everywhere
And it's not messy
It's creative
And before I met the love with you
All the houses burned
Except for one.
There was one house that remained
And it wasn't the same

But it wasn't stained either
We were allowed to light fresh candles
And both of us let us
And both of us let each other change
And both of us loved each other when we were lovers
And both of us held each other when we fell in love with others
And both of us forgave ourselves for the ways we burnt our bedrooms
And both of us chose to light the flame of friendship
Of a different type of love
A love that burnt through all the resistance
A love that said yes to not being sexy together but still both being sexy
And that being okay
And our partners being okay
And our lives being okay
And our loves being okay
And then there was you
And I keep trying to burn the house down
Even though I don't want to
Even though my soul says
'This is the one to keep house with'
Even though we have multiple houses
There's a little arsonist that lives inside me who says
Let it rip
Let it burn
Let the candle tip
Into the curtain
Let it take hold
Let it be reduced to ashes

And now
It doesn't matter
None of it matters
It's all just a symbol
Now the love is so real
It doesn't matter what happens to the house
Because the candle is in our hearts
Both of them
And the heart shared between us
The heart we both feed
The candle we both light
And sometimes it's the candle we both try to blow out
And it doesn't matter
Because there's always one of us there saying
It doesn't matter how hard you blow
This flame is evergreen
And it is
The flame is evergreen when the flame is the soul
– A soul cannot burn down

I remember when I figured out you were the one
I stepped into the world of imagination
And I imagined my most favourite life
The life that filled me with joy
The life with the light turned on
The life where I was a famous writer
And a world renowned singer
And a wonderful traveller
And a really great friend
And an empowering mother
And a sovereign woman
And a creative tigress
And really everything I'd ever wanted to be
And in my imagination
I could see myself in ways I'd never before let myself imagine
I'd see a beauty I'd never before seen manifest
I saw myself held in a grace I'd only believed to be in fairytales
And right there
In the peak of all of this vision
Right beside me
There was you
– And that was how I knew our fires were meant to burn together

They said getting married was what made it legit

It'll give us protection

It'll fit us in

It'll make everything make sense

It'll take it to the next level,

Yes it is different

It's a big commitment

It gives you rights over each other

It gives you rights together

It'll help for when you have children

It'll make it easier with splitting your property and assets

There will be tax benefits

And tax downfalls

Maybe you should and maybe you shouldn't

Maybe it's a terrible decision

Maybe nobody knows

Maybe it's outdated

Maybe marriage is broken

Maybe society is

Maybe marriage is for you

Hang on

Maybe now it doesn't matter

Maybe do a ritual

Maybe make promises

Maybe spend money on something else

Maybe have a huge party and invite everyone you've ever met

Maybe do what I did

Definitely do what I did

What I did was perfect, you'll love it

My mum said...

My dad said...

When I got married

I wouldn't ever do this...

I would for sure do that...

Everyone said a million things

And we said

There's a vision in our hearts

And that's what matters

And in our vision we are married and it's legal

And that's what matters

And here's what marriage means to us

And that's what matters

And here's what we are committing to

And that's what we choose

And there are a billion versions of other people's definitions

And here's ours

And that's what matters

And then in twelve weeks

The whole vision fell together

Because we told it to

And then we were married

And then the whole world changed

Because we chose it to

Because we chose the new phase

Because we chose what it means

And because we directed the fire
– A sovereign fire has longevity

I told my grandfather we were getting married
And he said
'It's a big commitment,
Are you ready for that?'
And we smiled
And we looked at each other
And we looked at him
And we said yes
And he left the room to get his tie
And he came back with a light on his face
And love in his eyes
And announced he didn't have any ties anymore
He'd given them up
He wouldn't wear them to any more funerals
– He bought a new tie to celebrate our marriage fire

When no one else is looking
And you are off asleep
And all the world is with you
Everybody off in dreams
And I'm sitting in my reading chair
Staring at the flames
The fireplace, it sings to me
Our future children's names
And even if we didn't have them
I'd still hear their songs
They'd be the children of our neighbours
And in lands so far from our shores
And still I'd hear their songs
And still I'd sit here thinking
There's no one else I'd rather raise the children with
There's no one else I'd rather love the world with
There's no one else I'd rather make magic with
And not because you're the only person in the world I could ever love
Or I'm the only one that could ever be for you
But because
– Our love is the fire we choose

If fires could be made out of anything

There wouldn't be anything left

There wouldn't be any point

There wouldn't be any learning

There wouldn't be any fulfilment in pursuing the truth

And maybe fires can be made from anything

And there are different types of fires

And there's a special type of fire that's made when you really choose a person

When you say,

Yes,

I love you,

And I choose to be with you,

And you declare to one another

This is the way that is true for us to be together,

And you see that in your souls,

And maybe there are more than two of you!

And it doesn't matter

Because this is the way the fires of your souls wish to burn

And you let them

And there's a different type of liberation available to you

When you let yourself soul love

When you let your souls guide the love

When the love goes beyond the body

Beyond the concept

Beyond the

Him

Her

One

Two

They

Them

Three

Four

Beyond the

Marriage

Boyfriend

Girlfriend

Partner

Special friend

Lover

Best friend

Beyond all the definitions

When the words matter so much less

Than the mutual understanding

And the world matters so much less

Than the mutual understanding

When the soul beats louder than words

And even if you can't be together

You close your eyes and you are

Because in your spirit there is a mutual understanding

And you know

You just know

And maybe that's the only fire that really matters

– Soul fire is the way

Maybe you've never met a soul fire
Or maybe you have
And you've never let it burn
Maybe you've decided
Soul fire isn't for you
Even if you'd really love it to be
Even if you long for it to be
Even if you wish for it to be
It all feels so far away
It all feels so cold and lonely
It all feels so terribly burnt down
Derelict
Unloved
Like you missed the moment
You missed the person
They were there and you had your eyes closed
You were going to meet them on that trip and you didn't go
You were going to see them and then they fell in love
I'd like you to remember
I urge you to remember
That when you have a dream
You are also in someone's dream
If you have a dream of a love
They are out there dreaming of you
And they may not know it yet
And maybe you don't either
But out there this person
Who could be your very next soul-firing person

Is living a life
Enjoying a life
Longing for a life with you
Wishing for a life with you
Hoping for a life with you
And all that longing, wishing, hoping will be for nothing
If you don't let the soul fire burn
And all you have to do
Is decide to let the soul fire burn
– Welcome the soul fire

Welcome the soul fire
Like a distant fond memory
Welcome the soul fire
Like an old friend returning
Welcome the soul fire
As if you already know it
As if it is familiar
And you will see
You do already know it
It is familiar
Because the soul fire is no secret
There is no special pilgrimage you must go on to find it
It is not trapped in a tomb in a mystery mountain
It is not beyond riddles and mazes in a foreign secret place
No
The soul fire is you
The soul fire isn't separate
The soul fire is right here
The soul fire is right now
It was always there
It is always going to be there
It is here
— Soul fire isn't created or destroyed, it just is

What if you remembered the soul fire was inside your heart right now?
What if you remembered every heart had a soul fire?
What if you were looking for it?
What if you allowed yourself to become one with it?
What if you stopped denying it?
What if you no longer needed to fix or find it?
What if it didn't matter what anyone else thought about it?
What if it didn't matter how it made anybody else feel?
What if all that mattered was that you remembered it?
What if the more you see it, the more you see it?
What if the more you receive it, the more you receive it?
What if the more you feel it, the more you feel it?
What if you don't need anything other than your soul fire?
What if you allowed your soul fire to burn what no longer serves you?
And what if you allowed it to burn away the debris gently?
What if the soul fire could soothe you?
What if the soul fire only ever burnt you if you asked it to in pursuit of your truth?
What if you watched your soul fire as a symbol of intuitive communication?
What if you listened to your soul fire as it spoke to you?
What if your lover turned on the soul fire all over your body?
What if your loved one noticed when the soul fire was flickering?
What if you made it your mission to turn on the soul fire you perceive as missing?
What if soul fire was everywhere you looked and some you were attracted to and some you weren't
And still you saw the power in all the soul fire?

What if soul fire is the way home to yourself?
– Yes, yes, yes soul fire

Yes

Can mean anything you want it to

And

No

Can mean anything you want it to

In your body

In your home

Because your body

Is your home

And there may be bits of your body

That don't fully represent your truth

And you could still say yes to loving them

And no to needing to fix them

And yes to the behaviour that would empower change in you

Not because you are saying no to your own flesh

Because you are saying yes to your own light

It is time

You noticed

To what you say yes

And to what you say no

And let yourself choose the soul fire

– If you're unsure, the soul fire will tell you

There's a myth
That says the soul fire lives in a certain place
And it's a helpful myth
Because it helps you form a relationship
It helps you start
It helps you say hello
But it isn't meant to limit your growth
It isn't meant to be a rule
It isn't meant to say, 'No it can't be like that'
It doesn't mean it can't be different
It just means
Start here
The myth can be helpful
As stories are helping
And learning through stories is very natural
And natural is easy
And easy is helpful
And easy gives us momentum
But your myth
Is different to the great myth
The myth of your soul fire has a specific pattern
And a specific story
And it is yours to tell
No one can tell you where to put your soul fire
And no one can really put it out
You have to say yes to smothering your flames
And you have to say no to brightening them
So stop living into someone else's myth

And write your own
You say hello
And then you tell your story
Eventually
You will walk yourself home
And the path will have been lit by your own flame
As no one else can do that for you
We can point to a torch
And we can encourage you to brighten it
But no
We cannot walk the walk
We can only fan a flame you allow to be fanned
We can only brighten the candle you hold out to us
Your soul fire is in you
And it's expression is on you
And I promise you that is good news
– Your soul fire is yours

Fire After Dark [Adults Only]
The Epilogue

He held me down
And I'm meant to like it
I can't breathe
And it's meant to be okay
I can't feel the skin on my arse anymore
The smacking is meant to be welcome
Apparently it's a compliment!
Nothing is wrong
I'll see him tonight
And her tomorrow
And they both know
And everyone is okay
And even though I'm so full
My schedule is so full
My diary is so full
My bed is so full
My life has so many options
There are so many willing participants
So many dance partners
And oh,
How I have danced
And how I will dance
And how I want to dance
And how I find that nothing good happens in the end
– Fire is discerning even if the human isn't

'Don't have sex unless you want to be them,'
My teacher said it
I didn't believe
Until I did
– Fire spreads whether you like it or not

Awakening in the bedroom
Is like trying a different food
It's been right there before you this whole time
And you never imagined it would taste this good
Yet of course you didn't
Because you didn't know any better or different
And it's okay
There's a peace that falls over you
For all the pain
And all the misunderstanding
And all the lovers who didn't know any better
And you realise
Even though the bodies are adults
We are essentially behaving like children
And that makes sense
Because adulthood is initiation
And you realise
That so is sex
And if you've done it without the recognition
If you've been dancing with no teacher
It's not all bad
It's not bad to freestyle
There's just a few things you might have missed
A few dance moves you thought you had to learn when really you didn't
And that's the funny thing about waking up in the bedroom
You realise it's less about learning
And doing

And dancing a performance
And more about being
And receiving
And giving
And playing
And feeling
And laughing
And crying
And screaming
And looking
And allowing
And guiding
And communicating
And asking
And telling
And letting energy speak louder than words
And letting words come anyway
And it's so much less about the right amount of pulling or kissing or smacking
And so much more about my soul meeting yours
– And suddenly the fire and the body is everything and nothing

When he touches me I am scared

When she touches me I am filled with anticipation

When they touch me it seems it should be the same

And it is so different

And on a different day a different touch could feel right

From a different person

Because it's less about the touch

And more about the vibration of it

And less about the him or her or they

And more about the fire

When the fires start to dance in my pelvis,

It's a yes

When the fires are like a starry open sky in my heart,

It's a yes

When the fires are as if an angel is caressing my head,

It's a yes

And when the fires start to melt together,

It's a full body yes

And the world melts away while we become one

And oh,

You can't help but fall in love

And now I know the difference between making love and having sex

We are the difference

The fire is the difference

The true

Burning

Moving

Spreading

Wild

Fire

– The fire can be everywhere if you let it

'Let's keep our clothes on,'
Your words dance in my ears
And I agree
I don't care about the clothes
I'm interested in the energy
I sit here
So close
And so far
From you
And you sit underneath and around me
So far
And so close
To me
With me
And it's as though the world never knew dancing before we knew this embrace
It's as though my cells are waking
The fire moves and says
Wake up body, this is love.
The fire transmutes and says
No more separating, we are one.
The fire transforms and says
We are remembering, let me love.
And my whole life I've been told the fire is wrong,
Now I've realised they were the ones missing the point
And it's my job to let everybody know
Gently
Loudly

Softly
True
Tell the people the truth
– Real fire lives in us all

I stand before you

Naked

Exposed

One

With the light that flickers from the candle

And the heat that pours from the fireplace

And the yearning that spreads

Groin to fingertips

I am here

Me

Alive

Ready

Open

Soft

Hard

Gentle

Strong

Ready

Open

Take me

– Make me one with your fire

'Come here,'
He looks me up and down in his imagination, I'm sure
But in real life he looks me in the eyes as I stand before him
Completely open
Completely revealed
Completely longing
'Look at me,'
I whisper
And I might as well yell
I see his eyes grow
His eyebrows raised
A smile small in movement that still reaches his eyes
And down those eyes go
Slowly
Hungrily
Patiently
Taking all of me in
Taking time
Taking so much time
I turn around
This is me
Full circle
His eyes stay with me
His hands open the sheets
His arms outstretched
I am on all fours
He is all around me
A gentle kiss

So soft it nearly didn't happen

I turn away

He pulls me in

We hold

Together in this love

United in this affection

I roll my hips

The invitation he was waiting for

His hands fall down with grace

Every touch awakening light in my body

Every poke less accidental

Everything is on the surface

Nothing physically penetrates

But the energy does

The energy goes inside me everywhere his hands are

I gasp

Quietly

This moment is just for us

He is kissing me all over

All

Over

And I love it

I lean in

I open

I dance

He moans

He loves it

He leans in

He wants more
He dances atop me
I whisper
'I don't think I can take anymore,'
He looks at me with loving delight
He knows I can
He knows I'm trying to withdraw from him
He doesn't let me
'You'll have to.'
He says it and yet I know it's completely my choice
He's reading what I want
He's right
He dives back in
I am consumed by him
Until I become one with him
The fireworks are different now
They're all over my body
Electrifying the entire bedroom field
Animals with hearts bleeding
Eyes crying
He climbs up my body
Softly
Slowly
I am so sensitive
Little touches shaking
Shivers
Alive
He kisses me

He waits at the window
The window is open
There is no glass to shatter
He has removed the wall
There's nothing left but for my yes
'Yes,'
I whisper
Though looking at him would have been enough
He enters
And waits
Gently in
Then out
Then deeply in
Then waits
We breathe
We gaze
His face changes
A leopard
An Egyptian
'I remember you,'
I say it to him
'I keep nearly saying, "I love you"'
I say it out loud
'I love you too'
He knows
We love each other
We have loved each other before
We are loving each other now

His sword touches my heart
Every time
In
And the bottom of my heart opens
In
And the front of my heart opens even more
In
And the stars in my chest fly into his
In
And the stars travel down his body
In
And it's waking all of his stars
In
And the fires of a thousand stars dance between us
In
And my definition of the heart has crumbled
In
And I know that this is love
In
And I know nothing
In
And tears fall into his caressing
In
And sex will never be without love again
In
And that is how I met you
– When the fires of one soul recognise another

It didn't matter,

That he wasn't my forever person

He taught me

That a forever love

Doesn't have to look like what we are told

I will love him forever

And he is not my one

My one came like a slowly crashing wave

My one washed over me in moments of tranquillity

My one was less fire and more healing lotion

Less explosion and more lava dripping

And still

She explodes me

And still

She draws me in

And still

She waits with anticipation

And still

She reads the signals

And still

She dances atop

And still

There is nothing else needed

And still

The shapeshifting

And now

My own shapeshifting

And still

I wait for her
When she is ready we dance
And no one knows the way the world bends
But I'm sure everyone feels it
Maybe they don't know
Our love is changing the world
Likely they never will
Definitively, it'll never matter
It's already happened
– When the fire comes home, everybody feels it

There were others I'd thought were the one
So how do I know the difference?
Peace
Peace is how
And not the kind of peace you've been taught about
Where everything is okay
And there's never any fighting
No more conflict
No
That's not real peace
Peace is when the whole world can happen
Everything can be going all at once
Nothing can be going the way we expected
Everything can be different
A million actions making a billion chain reactions
And still together is the path
Not because we need each other
Not because we couldn't walk the path alone
Not because we are anxiously together
But because there is a calling
And how does one hear the calling?
One may ask this grand question
And one might say in response
When your lights touch you shine brighter
And so do they
And so too will the world
 – Fire is the light inside you that tells you to love

Water River Run
out June 2025

A drop of WATER

When the cold comes
It may be startling
It may be everything you wanted
And more
It may be terror-filled
Chill you to the bones
It may be moving
Awakening you with eroticism
Or it may melt you
Into a puddle of grief
Until you are so shaken
That you must remember
That the water isn't cold
And neither are you
The water is simply water
The water is what you are made of
And it's only cold because you're telling it, 'No,'
– You are supposed to feel

ELLIE ANN DEIGHTON

Not all water is running
Read ***Water River Run*** from June 2025

About the author

I teach humans how to live in the light of their true selves and I go first.

Like an integrity radar

Through life

Mine and yours

I will find the cracks

And spit them out

Until our world tastes like honey together

For I am not here to walk alone

And neither are you.

It is no mistake that you are here reading this.

Is it that the stories in my books are calling you in for a journey?

Is my music singing you home to the Temple of You?

Is my curriculum asking you to become more of yourself?

Is now the time?

I believe so.

The scientist in me has a hypothesis,

That you are magic,

The facilitator in me

Can prove it,

The witch in me

Can give you the tools to cast it,
The woman in me
Can celebrate you as you shine,
The artist in me
Is on stage creating beside you.
You are magic,
And here,
You will find that you are home.
– about Ellie, author of **Fire Body Warm**

Author's note

You are never alone
Because you will always be one with fire
And fire will always be one with you
And you can close your eyes and see the fire
And you can open your eyes and look for the fire
And you can place your hands on your pelvis and feel the fire
And you can sing a song and hear the fire
And even on the darkest days
There can be a light
Because of the fire
And the greatest gift you could ever give yourself
Is to learn to
See
Listen
Feel
Receive
Remember
Play
Speak
Be

Your
Fire
– Fire is what I teach

And I can teach you fire too
Or you can receive my firey notes straight into your inbox

Subscribe to the fire at elliedeighton.com/fire

Acknowledgements

Clare

Nicolas

Mitch

Erica

Callum

Ilse

Kara

Chantelle

Antosh

Tara

Georgia

Alex

Lo

Jacqlin

William

Veenu

Mem

Paige

Alaina

Luke

Swaziland
– Thank you for showing me your soul fire, ***Fire Body Warm*** wouldn't exist without you

www.ingramcontent.com/pod-product-compliance
Lightning Source LLC
Chambersburg PA
CBHW071720020426
42333CB00017B/2336